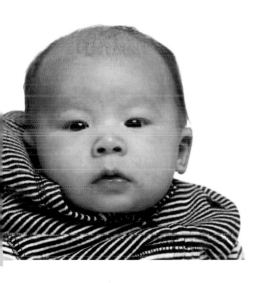

Published by East West Discovery Press
P.O. Box 3585, Manhattan Beach, CA 90266
Phone: 310-545-3730, Fax: 310-545-3731
Website: www.eastwestdiscovery.com

Author: Crystal Smith
Photographer: Michael Satoshi Garcia
Art Direction: Crystal Smith
Design and Production: Crystal Smith, Jennifer Thomas

ISBN-13: 978-0-9913454-6-5 Hardcover
Library of Congress Cataloging-in-Publication Data Available
First Trilingual English, Spanish, and Chinese Edition 2016
Published in the United States of America
Printed in China

A Trilingual Book in English, Spanish, & Chinese

I am
Hapa!

我是 Hapa! ¡Soy Hapa!

Author/Autora/作者
Crystal Smith

Photographer/Fotógrafo/摄影师
Michael Satoshi Garcia

East West Discovery Press
Manhattan Beach, California

I am Hapa, and I am unique.

Soy hapa y soy único.

我是 Hapa, 我很独特。
wǒ shì Hapa, wǒ hěn dú tè

I am Hapa,
and I speak two languages.

Soy hapa
y hablo dos idiomas.

我是 Hapa,

wǒ shì Hapa,

我会说两种语言。
wǒ huì shuō liǎng zhǒng yǔ yán

I am Hapa,
and I love my creamy skin.

Soy hapa
y me encanta mi piel sedosa.

我是 Hapa,

wǒ shì Hapa,

我爱我光滑的皮肤。

wǒ ài wǒ guāng huá de pí fū

I am Hapa,
and I eat all kinds of food.

Soy hapa
y como toda clase de alimentos.

我是 Hapa,

wǒ shì Hapa,

我吃各种食物。

wǒ chī gè zhǒng shí wù

I am Hapa,
and I love to share.

Soy hapa
y me encanta compartir.

我是 Hapa,

wǒ shì Hapa,

我喜欢分享。

wǒ xǐ huān fēn xiǎng

I am Hapa,
and I love my silly smile.

Soy hapa
y me encanta mi sonrisa tonta.

我是 Hapa,

wǒ shì Hapa,

我爱我滑稽的笑容。

wǒ ài wǒ huá jī de xiào róng

I am Hapa, and I love
my awesome hair.

Soy hapa y me encanta
mi cabello increíble.

我是 Hapa,

wǒ shì Hapa,

我爱我超酷的头发。

wǒ ài wǒ chāo kù de tóu fǎ

I am Hapa, and I love
taking care of others.

Soy hapa y me encanta
cuidar de los demás.

我是 Hapa,
wǒ shì Hapa,
我喜欢照顾别人。
wǒ xǐ huān zhào gù bié rén

I am Hapa, and I am special
inside and out.

Soy hapa y soy especial
por dentro y por fuera.

我是 Hapa,

wǒ shì Hapa,

我從內到外都很特別。

wǒ cóng lǐ dào wài dōu hěn tè bié.

I am Hapa,
and I love my beautiful family.

Soy hapa
y amo a mi hermosa familia.

我是 Hapa,

wǒ shì Hapa,

我爱我美好的家庭。

wǒ ài wǒ měi hǎo de jiā tíng

Big thanks to the amazing families
who made this book possible.

Un enorme agradecimiento a las familias increíbles
que hicieron posible la realización de este libro.

由衷感谢文中诸多美满家庭
yóu zhōng gǎn xiè wén zhōng zhū duō měi mǎn jiā tíng

协助本书出版成功
xié zhù běn shū chū bǎn chéng gōng

—Crystal Smith

Author/Autora/作者
Crystal Smith

Photographer/Fotógrafo/摄影师
Michael Satoshi Garcia